Weather Wise

Rain

Helen Cox Cannons

Heinemann
LIBRARY
Chicago, Illinois

© 2015 Heinemann Library
an imprint of Capstone Global Library, LLC
Chicago, Illinois

All rights reserved. No part of this publication may be
reproduced or transmitted in any form or by any means,
electronic or mechanical, including photocopying,
recording, taping, or any information storage and retrieval
system, without permission in writing from the publisher.

Edited by Siân Smith and John-Paul Wilkins
Designed by Philippa Jenkins and Peggie Carley
Picture research by Ruth Blair
Production by Victoria Fitzgerald
Originated by Capstone Global Library Ltd

Library of Congress Cataloging in Publication Data
Cataloging-in-publication information is on file with the Library
of Congress.
ISBN 978-1-4846-0545-5 (hardcover)
ISBN 978-1-4846-0555-4 (paperback)
ISBN 978-1-4846-0570-7 (eBook PDF)
ISBN 978-1-4846-2484-5 (saddle stitch)

Photo Credits
Corbis: Steve Cole/Anyone/amanaimages, cover; Dreamstime:
Egonzitter, 22, Hassanmohiudin, 4, Qwasyx, 18; iStockphoto:
aimintang, 14, 23 (bottom), IsaacLKoval, 6, 23 (top), Krakozawr, 5,
oriba, 20; Shutterstock: Balazs Kovacs, 21, Charlie Edward, 11, 23
(second from bottom), Dirk Ott, 10, Huansheng Xu, 7, leospek,
9, Matej Hudovernik, 8, 23 (middle), Viorel Sima, 15; SuperStock:
Lisette Le Bon, 19

We would like to thank John Horel for his invaluable help in the
preparation of this book.

Every effort has been made to contact copyright holders of
material reproduced in this book. Any omissions will be rectified
in subsequent printings if notice is given to the publisher.

Printed in the United States   6472

Contents

What Is Rain? 4

Types of Rain. 6

How Does Rain Form? 12

What Do You Wear in
  Rainy Weather?. 18

How Does Rain Help Us? 20

Did You Know? 22

Picture Glossary 23

Index 24

Notes for Parents and Teachers 24

What Is Rain?

Rain is water that falls from clouds.

Rain feels wet on your skin.

Types of Rain

When rain falls, it can be light rain. This is sometimes called **drizzle**.

When rain falls, it can be heavy rain.
This is sometimes called a downpour.

7

In some places, it does not rain for a long time. There is not enough water.

This is called a **drought**.

In some places, it rains for a long time. There is too much water.

This is called a **flood**.

How Does Rain Form?

One raindrop is made from tiny drops of water. Each tiny drop is called a **droplet**.

When the Sun warms water, some of the water becomes a gas. This gas is called **vapor**.

Vapor comes from oceans, rivers, and lakes. Vapor even comes from puddles.

Vapor also comes from plants and animals. We usually cannot see this vapor.

15

The vapor rises into the air. Then it cools down and turns into droplets. The droplets make clouds.

The droplets join together and form raindrops. When the raindrops get too heavy, they fall to the ground.

What Do You Wear in Rainy Weather?

When it rains, you could wear
a raincoat.

18

When it rains, you could also
use an umbrella.

How Does Rain Help Us?

Rain brings water back down to Earth. It keeps the oceans filled.

Rain helps plants grow.

Did You Know?

Forests that have a lot of rain are called rain forests.

Picture Glossary

drizzle light rain

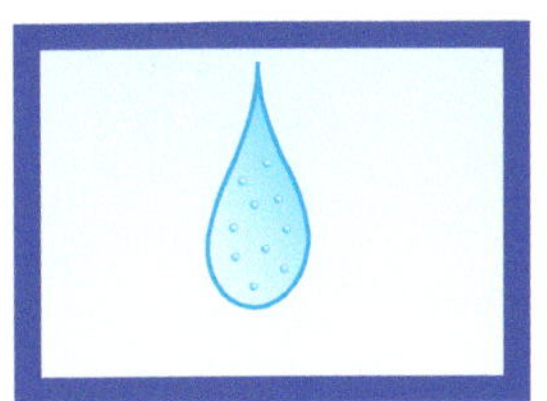

droplet tiny drop of water

drought long period without rainfall

flood large amount of water that spreads over dry land

vapor gas created by heating water

Index

animal 15

cloud 4, 16

droplet 12 ,16, 17, 23

plant 15, 21

vapor 13, 14, 15, 16, 23

Notes for Parents and Teachers

Before Reading
Assess background knowledge. Ask: What is rain? How does rain form? How does rain help us?

After Reading
Recall and reflection: Ask children if their ideas about rain at the beginning were correct. What new facts about rain did they learn?

Sentence knowledge: Ask children to look at page 13. How many sentences are on the page? Have them point to the beginning and end of one sentence.

Word recognition: Have children point at the word *some* on page 8 and 10. Can they think of another word that means about the same as *some*?